Victory at Lepanto
Don Juan's Campaign to Save Christendom

By Francisco Nervantes

Prologue

At the court of Charles V, Holy Roman Emperor; where Charles admits contrition to his son Philip at Charles' own infidelity.

"Philip, my son, even though you are only twenty years old, one day soon, you will be King of Spain. My responsibility is to guide you in such a way to help you to avoid my sinful, lustful ways. We must overcome strong personal desires, as we are held to a higher standard precisely because the people always look to our example. You must always remember the principle of Noblesse Oblige. To the extent that we wish to sow the seeds of a faithful Christian kingdom, we need to abide faithfully ourselves to the tenets of our faith.

Hence, though we hold high office, indeed because we hold high office, we must always be vigilant role models for our subjects.

As you know, your half-brother Don Juan, is born of my less-than perfect life. As such, he begins life with the stigma of being a bastard child. Nonetheless, he too must be guided by God's will. He will suffer greatly for this stigma, but with you as his role model and guide, he may very well redeem himself and me for my transgressions. Though I have been far from perfect, I am certainly contrite and will that you work together with him for the greater good.

We are not like the English or Normans who grasp at any hint of royal lineage. Don Juan must never be deluded into thinking that he can be King. He will need to earn all and anything that he aspires to in life. While you must not mistreat him, your oversight must necessarily be a strict one."

Meanwhile, Don Juan is with his young playmates at court including Riccardo, son of Philip's special advisor for the Spanish territories in the New World, Don Alvaro.

"Don Juan, you are not a real member of the royal family. My father, Don Alvaro, says that you should be sent to the new world where you can prove yourself."

Responding to Riccardo, "I will gladly demonstrate my chivalry by going to the new world. After all, it was my great grandparents who gave Cristobal Colon the charter to explore and bring Christianity to the New World."

Riccardo tells him "Ah, just as well, you are too fat to be a knight; maybe the rigors of the new world will help to reduce your weight so that you can return as a knight in shining armor!"

While the other boys are all laughing heartily, Don Juan retorts,

"You will see, someday I will prove my worth by conquering a great foe."

Laughing, Riccardo says "you will need to be a knight of the kingdom first and I don't think that your half-brother, the King shares your optimism. He sees you as more of a burden, having to feed that frame of yours!"

Ricardo and Don Juan begin to battle it out not with words but with their fists. Don Juan getting belted and pummeled by the older, stronger and more agile Ricardo. As Ricardo wrestles Don Juan to the ground, punching him all the way, the other boys chime in to ridicule Don Juan.

"What a poor excuse you are for a knight", you'll never be able to defeat even a single opponent let alone lead a great army in Victory."

Another boy Tomaso, chimes in, "Yeah, who wants a bastard kid to lead them into the breach against a formidable foe. I prefer a lowly but brave peasant to a fake royal."

Don Juan is overwhelmed by the expressions of disdain from his peers. No matter how he tries he is often ridiculed and ostracized. His birth status, his weight and Philip's refusal to school him in the tradition of nobility or royalty result in retreat to a preference for a solitary existence.

As Don Juan recedes further into depression and loneliness, feeling sorry for himself to the point of despair, he retreats to the monastery where his father Charles, is enduring his last days.

Charles tells Don Juan, "My son, the transgressions of a father need not be prologue of inferiority for the son. You must overcome Philip's taciturn nature and realize your own calling. The Lord has destined you for something which has not yet been revealed. You must allow yourself to participate fully in this manifest destiny."

"But how my lord, no one will give me a chance!"

"It's up to you, to find your way."

As the children of the royal court gather for their games, Don Juan is frequently missing, preferring to remain at the monastery where the monks, who are too busy with their own gardening, brewing and worship to pay much attention to him. Nonetheless their rhythmic discipline influences him to fast; depriving himself of the indulgences that he previously enjoyed.

He has secretly watched as the Abbot who leads all the monks has struggled with his own faith and prayed before the altar – "Lord, I believe, help my unbelief" as he prays before the Tabernacle deep into the early hours of the morning.

Such mortification on the part of the senior monk of the monastery has caused Don Juan to realize that he must humbly follow the example of the Abbot.

While Don Juan secretly donates his meals to the poor, he still has a longing to overcome the disdain of his peers. He aspires to the military greatness that his father Charles, the Holy Roman Emperor has hinted at. While on the one hand, developing his humility, he nonetheless wants to be recognized as chivalrous. He longs for the military glory which will justify his existence.

At fourteen, he rejoins the games of his peers at court and with quite a different profile.

Riccardo, as the leader of the group, sneers as Don Juan makes his reappearance among the children of the court. Rushing to tackle

Don Juan, Riccardo tries to pummel Don Juan as he was accustomed to doing.

"Little Juanito, just because you have been hiding out in the monastery, don't think that we won't continue to beat on you!"

But now Don Juan is much more fit and fights back.

As they fight to a draw, Riccardo tells Don Juan; "Obviously, you have been doing a lot more than just perfecting your soul, you are no longer a fat foe, but a worthy rival – let's see how you do when it comes to riding and competing in a joust!".

The kids at court continue to taunt Don Juan, but as he grows and matures, he is determined to overcome their taunts.

At the annual Royal Joust, there is a special time when the up and coming prospective knights, the children of courtiers, vie for the title of Child Champion.

Riccardo, realizing that Don Juan, by his fifteenth birthday, has become a formidable foe, has hatched a plot with his cohorts.

Riccardo urges Tomaso, "Amigo, we cannot let Don Juan prevail! He has no preordained right to be champion. Indeed, we are obligated to prevent him from achieving success! With his newly found prowess, he presents a challenge to our leadership among the kids at court."

Tomas responding, "Querido Riccardo, you know that Don Juan has been under the influence of monastic Dominicans for quite some time now. It is alleged that among the Dominicans, is a former champion who has trained him in much more than just spiritual matters. Indeed, they say that Don Juan has learned to joust from a master formerly known as Antonio of Andalusia. Antonio had been Charles' own champion right up until the death of the Holy Roman Emperor! Ever since then Antonio entered and has resided at the monastery. They say that he has much to repent, as he mortally wounded many a man. Only God will ever know if the men he killed were deserving of death!"

Don Juan is next seen riding from the Monastery on his way to the Joust. He emerges as a tall and lean figure, youthfully handsome and confident at his newly developed ability to compete for the title of Child Champion. The young women are breathless at his appearance in shining gold and red armor.

Dismounting, he kneels before his brother the King.

"My Lord King Philip, I beg your blessing for this combat on which I seek to glorify our father's name!"

"My little brother, you will always have my Blessing; we await the great challenge that you face in battling against such superior, more experienced foes."

Don Juan blesses himself as he arises to remount his horse.

One after another his tournament triumphs mount, increasing his pride and confidence to the point of vainglory.

Finally, Don Juan prepares for the ultimate joust of the tournament against his arch foe, Riccardo, who is one year his elder and in his last year of competition for the title of Child Champion. Only a year ago Riccardo had been defeated for the title and he is determined that he would not be denied again.

Riccardo, Tomaso and Jose secretly pay off the stable manager to grease the stirrups of Don Juan's Horse. They know that the traditional custom is for the championship contestants to walk their horses into the arena as an act of humility; only mounting their horses just before they ride.

Immediately after receiving their blessing from the King, Riccardo and Don Juan walk their horses to their starting point.

Mounting his steed, Don Juan immediately notices that he has been handicapped. With a shriek he charges forward but begins to slide from the saddle.

The crowd groans as they view his perceived fear! As Riccardo charges forward, he lands a powerful blow to the off-balance Don Juan, knocking him to the ground and claiming the title of Child Champion. While Don Juan writhes in pain Riccardo revels in the cheers of the crowd proclaiming him the winner.

Back at the monastery, Don Juan exclaims to Brother Antonio, "I will avenge this treachery! Riccardo and his minions have rigged our contest and I cannot allow such unfairness to prevail."

Bother Antonio replies, "But my dear Don Juan, of course you know that vengeance belongs to God alone."

Ironically, Riccardo has matured enough to realize that he was wrong to claim victory at all costs and under false pretenses.

Meanwhile, Riccardo confesses to Jose and Tomas, "My friends, I have wrongly claimed the title, I will express my contrition to Don Juan, and proclaim him true champion and my undying service to the Throne."

This is however unbeknownst to Don Juan, who's righteous indignation is raging.

While acknowledging Brother Antonio, Don Juan plots to avenge his sabotage.

Ironically, as Riccardo set out during the night to seek Don Juan's forgiveness, Don Juan rides out to meet his foe. Making it appear that he is being robbed, Don Juan engages Riccardo yelling "Robber."

Before Riccardo can explain, Don Juan lashes out at Riccardo with his sword. Not realizing his newly found power, Don Juan's blows to the unsuspecting Riccardo are accidentally fatal!

As bystanders gather in the darkness, Don Juan points to Riccardo as a would-be Robber. He is perceived as having made the innocent mistake of believing that he was about to be assaulted.

When later told by Jose and Tomas that Riccardo was en route to seek his forgiveness Don Juan breaks down in tears.

Don Juan to Tomas and Jose not realizing that they had participated in the plot to handicap his effort, Don Juan begs, "Tomas, why would so great a competitor as Riccardo feel the need to handicap my horse? His chances of winning were better than even."

Tomas answers, "Don Juan, Riccardo had already lost before and he knew that you have been trained, not just by anyone but by Antonio himself. Riccardo, therefore seemed to believe that you had more on your side than just physical prowess but also a supernatural aid. He may have felt that this was an advantage that was insurmountable."

Distraught, and completely contrite, Don Juan subsequently sets out on pilgrimage for Santiago de Compostela.

Arriving to his destination, he meets the French Ambassador to Spain, Jacques de Vincentian.

Jacques says to Don Juan, "My Dear Don, you should know that Francis, King of France, has confided in me his desire to meet you. His own father was killed in a jousting accident and recognized that you were almost killed in an unfortunate display of treachery at your own court."

Don Juan questions Jacques, "Monsieur Ambassador, I am only the bastard half-brother of Philip, why would your good King Francis entertain such a lowly person?"

Jacques tells Don Juan, "My Lord the King wishes to establish a rapport such that peace among Christian nations can be pursued. The tearing asunder of Christendom from the inside makes it so much more vulnerable to attack from the outside that my King understands the need to repair our friendship. In order to reunite the Thrones of Christendom he has asked me to relay to you an invitation to his upcoming nuptials to Mary Queen of Scots!"

Don Juan, acceding to the French Ambassador's invitation, arrives at Notre Dame Cathedral to attend the Nuptial Mass of the young Monarchs, Mary and Francis.

The Te Deum is sung and after Mass a great banquet ensues where Francis and his young bride entertain their counterpart from Spain.

Mary greets Don Juan, "My Lord, bienvenido a nuestra pais." As Mary was well-educated and spoke fluent Spanish, Don Juan was greatly comforted and felt at home in a foreign land.

Don Juan is also enchanted at Mary's beauty; her kindness and devout ways also gave him great hope. Due to her fluency in French as well as her native English, tradition is broken as she is asked to give the invocation blessing over the banquet.

"My dear friends, I beg the blessing of Almighty God on the food that we eat this evening. As many of you know, since I was born on December 8th, I was named after another Queen, one who never

reigned on earth, but reigns on the Throne of Angels in Heaven, Mary the Mother of our Lord and Savior Jesu Cristo! May they always guide us as we serve their people on earth on the way to their Heavenly Kingdom! Through Christ our Lord."

Mary's clear devotion to service had a significant impact on Don Juan. He was able to see beyond the small world where he had lived unto this point and his horizons were now greatly expanded. He looked up to Mary as she was a year or two older than he, but so much more informed, aware and devout. She had been born in Great Britain but her upbringing at the French court under the guidance of her Father in law, Henry II, King of France had an outsized influence on her intellectual and spiritual development.

This meeting with Don Juan, would be a premonition of things to come. It leads Don Juan to recognize that perhaps he could be an important part of the peacemaking process among Christian kingdoms. He thought, this could be the beginning of the cooperation much needed among the Thrones of Christendom. This could be the mission that his father, Charles V, Holy Roman Emperor had alluded to….

Back at the Spanish Court, after attending the wedding, Don Juan began to grow into the world view that would become his lasting legacy. Reporting back to his brother Philip, Don Juan says, "My Lord King, representing you at the Royal Wedding of Mary and Francis was an honor beyond words. Their Royal Highnesses, like you, especially Mary, are not only elegant, but much more importantly, erudite in their profound understanding of Noblesse Oblige. Their acknowledgement of the Heavenly Kingdom was truly inspirational. I now see clearly, that our father wisely planted within me, the seed of desire to help restore unity among the thrones of Christendom.

Philip, recognizing that his younger brother is coming of age, tells him, "Don Juan, you have begun to understand my many challenges in the world. Ultimately, the squabbles among the royal courts of Christendom will pale compared to the misery of conquest that the people of Europe will suffer if we fail to respond adequately to the external forces arrayed against us. The people of Europe will be enslaved to an intolerant new master; one that sneers at the example of Christ our true King! This would be the ultimate tragedy, and it could very well occur on our watch if we fail to do just as you have said."

I The Cause

In the dark of a near moonless night the foreboding hulks of the Grand Turkish Galleys at Lepanto, though moored, bobbed up and down in the waves. Onboard there is lashing of Christian slaves. Two slaves, in particular, who tried to escape and lead a rebellion in order to help the Christians at Famagusta (where there was a massacre of men, women and children *__after__* they had surrendered under a white flag of truce), are singled out for the ultimate torture.

The Turkish officer commanding one of the vessels, in the presence of the ship's crew commands his executioner – "These Christians thought not only that they could escape but that they would live to fight us another day. We must let them be an example to their protégés that the only way to live will be under our subjugation and rule. If they object, as these have done, we will subject them to swift and immediate recrimination and indeed execution. These slaves must do our bidding in fighting against their own brethren. What better way to train their kind for our ultimate conquest of all Europe?"

The lashing and screaming of the captured Christians serving as galley slaves can be heard among the other vessels of the Turkish fleet.

"Now cut their heads off for all to see!"

It was the 6th of June 1571 and King Philip II of Spain was convening his closest advisors amidst the Gardens and exterior beauty of the Escorial Palace. The voice of Philip is heard faintly echoing down a long dark corridor of the Escorial to find Philip in a large room at a 'round table' with his Advisory Council. Among those assembled are his half-brother Prince **Don Juan**, Admiral Giandrea Doria; the Marques of Santa Cruz (Don Alvaro), the old, partially paralyzed Don Garcia de Toledo and Don Luis Requesens.

They are having a discussion regarding battle planning to prevent the Grand Turk from further pillaging and conquering the entire Mediterranean.

No sooner had they closed the door to begin their discussion when a messenger arrives at the Escorial to bring the news that the Venetians have finally signed the treaty of alliance to combat the Grand Turk – Selim the Sot.

Philip is at first joyous at the good news; looks up after reading the communiqué from the messenger and somberly says – "The Venetians have paid a heavy price – many have been taken into slavery, even lost their lives at the hands of the Turk.

Now that we are formally allied with the Venetians by virtue of this agreement, we will join forces to put an end to their horrible torment from the Middle East. I will finally commit the great Spanish fleet that we have been assembling – and you – my brother Don Juan, with a special Papal blessing, will command the Armada.

Nonetheless, the caveat is that you must agree to take under advisement, the wise counsel and guidance of Admiral Giandrea Doria. You must agree to defer to his advice as you would mine – for he is a great Admiral of the ocean sea who knows the treacherous waters of the Mediterranean as well as the clever, crushing tactics of the Turk.

My Lords, this will be a dangerous mission in which your forces are likely to be greatly outnumbered. The skill of the Grand Turk and his minions neither should be ***dismissed nor taken lightly***. You must know and recall that the inhumanity, treachery and terror with which the renegade Turks have fanned out across an ever-expanding horizon – must be stopped once and for all."

Don Juan, sensing his destiny for glory approaching rapidly upon him, beseeched his brother the King "My Sovereign Lord, now you can no longer refrain from telling your commanders what horrible agonies the Turks have been inflicting – upon the innocents far and wide all across the Mediterranean. Indeed, we cannot shrink from the admonition received from our Father on his death bed."

They both simultaneously flashback to the deathbed of the Holy Roman Emperor – Charles V – their father.

In their mind's eye, Philip and Prince Don Juan both see the Emperor as he lies drawing his last earthly breaths, tells his Son the King - and his stepbrother Don Juan, always to uphold the True faith; ministering to the poor and defending the people from evil.

King Philip reminded his councilors that the Turks had been terrorizing the Mediterranean for the past forty years – since Philip and Don Juan's father Charles had defeated the previous Sultan's forces at the (Turkish) siege on Vienna.

So great was Sulieman the Sultan's desire to conquer Europe that he assembled one of the greatest invasion forces of all time to attack Vienna as the first stage of his planned assault on Europe.

Indeed, it was forty-two years prior, that the young (newly-crowned) Sultan Sulieman's men landed on European shores to begin his first major campaign as Sultan."

Don Juan begs Philip, "My Lord King, tell us again of the chivalry of our father in risking his own life on the front lines in fighting the Turk to a stalemate in defense of Vienna.

"My young brother is correct; my commanders – you should hearken well from the inspiration of our father Charles – who suffered near fatal wounds in personally defending Vienna from being overrun by Sulieman's forces. In fact, the day after being wounded, as he rode out onto the battlefield, the Turks were rumored to have believed that El Cid himself had been reincarnated to fight again. Their spirit was broken, and they were never able to rally again against the city."

Meanwhile, unbeknownst to the Turks, Vienna had nearly been brought to its knees by their siege. Nonetheless, the city was saved by the heroic acts of Charles and his men. Shortly thereafter he was named Holy Roman Emperor, leader of the Hapsburg dynasty and **<u>Defender of the Faith</u>**.

"My brother **Don** Juan, it falls on your shoulders to carry out the tradition to which our father dedicated his life."

Philip's commanders, filled with inspiration, all nodded in agreement.

"While I wish I could be with you, affairs of state require me to remain here. Just yesterday I received word of the precarious situation of our cousin Mary Queen of Scots. There is, so as you see, much to be done on the home front among our sister nations, organizing, indeed preserving – the integrity of efforts so that the enemy cannot conquer through division - which is obviously their intention! To wit – we must now set our strategy for defending the Mediterranean.

Don Alvaro, would you now report on the intelligence that your **spies** in the court of the Turk have uncovered.”

“Yes, my Lord Philip - as we speak, the Turk is planning a full-scale assault on the Mediterranean. This time though, rather than pick a single point for siege as with Vienna or Malta - their plan is to probe along a much larger **route** in order to find the nearest weak point for further exploitation.

Their top Admirals from Mustapha Ali **Pasha** to Barbarossa, the King of evil himself, have already been deployed with orders to attack, pillage and plunder; all the while concealing the main point of attack. So varied are the plans that my spies have not determined where the main pressure points will come!”

Meanwhile, **<u>Don Juan</u>** had secretly employed his own sources of intelligence.

Don Juan elaborates, “My Lord, there is word that among the main attack points will be Tunis and Malta- so as to achieve staging grounds for a main assault on Venice – and then even the Eternal City – Rome itself!”

My brother, “Our father himself gave the isle of Malta to the knights of St. John; there will never be surrender on Malta; we will defend it to the death of the last man!”

 Philip then listened attentively to Don Alvaro as well as to his half-brother Don Juan. Their concept was to counterattack wherever they encountered the enemy.

Nonetheless, Philip was reluctant to split the force for fear of playing into the enemy's hands.

Philip points out, "Don Juan, my brother, there is deception inherent in these intelligence reports; with the goal of having us split our forces; we must not be drawn into this temptation!

Our forces must remain united.

Admittedly, our Armada's flanks must always be protected from marauding corsairs – such that we are always least vulnerable from being surprised and overwhelmed by the enemy's main assault force.

Gentlemen, there is another even more foreboding reason why we must not split our force; **why we must not fail.**

There is reason to believe that the Turk has set sail with a highly secret and devastating new weapon.

They say that this new weapon can tear down the walls of our mighty fortresses or destroy twenty ships of the line with one salvo. Hence, we have yet another reason to be always in position to defer to Admiral Doria's seamanship- we must not fail in destroying the force which transports weapons of such mass destructive power!

Our strategy will be to probe where we may, eradicating the enemy where we have superior strength, defending in unison, our gains and lands, all the while seeking to give battle to the enemy's main assault force of ships and troops."

Philip though deeply somber, was greatly strengthened by the memory of his father and the Emperor's dying words.

He gathered his wits and began to summarize the meeting with the words; "I'm afraid that I now have no choice but to apprise you all fully of the atrocities which have been occurring with ever-increasing frequency and ferocity. I could not before this, for fear of unleashing an angry mob which would have been just another group of disorganized (and ultimately defeated) Defenders of our honor and way of life.

Our new alliance will now serve as the gathering force to unleash the combined righteous fury of Spain, Venice and the Papal and other Italian states. The course that we now find ourselves on is the natural response to ***the massacre of the men, women and children <u>under the white flag</u> at Famagusta on the Island of Cyprus. This was to be the beginning of the Turk's renewed reign of terror throughout the Mediterranean***; though this time the terror was not for the sake of terror alone but rather for the conquest of all Christendom!"

II – Servant of the Servants of God

Cardinal Pio – having entered the Dominican Order at the very early age of 14, now as a Cardinal; attends the Papal Conclave of 1565, after the death of Pope Pius IV.

Pio is under the spiritual guidance of Cardinal Charles Borromeo – at the Funeral of Pope Pius IV.

Cardinal Pio points out, "My dear Cardinal Borromeo, your Uncle, Pius IV, was a good Pope whose idea it was to reconvene and complete the work of the Council of Trent in the face of many difficulties and overwhelming adversity."

Cardinal Borromeo replies, "It's true, Pio that the Holy Spirit inspired him to reassemble the Council. With the guidance of the spirit we have been able to achieve a consensus among a very learned group for the passage of these important doctrinal reforms. This was no small accomplishment. Nonetheless, as a Medici, he was from a secular background. The church must now have a leader with a spiritual approach in order to implement well these reform principles in a pastoral way."

Cardinal Pio says, "The Holy Spirit, as always, will guide the selection process."

Cardinal Borromeo, pondering Pio's reply deeply says, "There is a certain pastoralism in your view, Pio…"

Pio, with a look of incredulity replies, "Your eminence, you must not be insinuating…. I am a humble servant who wishes only to return to the flock which needs me…."

Cardinal Borromeo, cutting off Pio says, "Yes, my brother cardinal – that is precisely the point…."

At *the Installation of Pius V as Pope –*

Pope Pius V *(formerly Cardinal Pio), with great humility;* My brother cardinals, may God forgive you for what you have done in electing me;

Nonetheless, I accept this enormous burden only with great reticence – since I do not yet share your view that this is a result of the Spirit at work among us. With your help, we will strive to bring souls home to the Lord – all the while trying to help alleviate earthly evil and destitution."

Outside – White Smoke rises from the chimney of St Peter's Basilica!

The crowd below cheers – as His Holiness, Pope Pius V – steps out on to the balcony.

III – Communion with Rome

Given the critical, even desperate situation prevailing in the Mediterranean, it was not surprising that one of the new pope's very first official acts was to receive the Ambassador from the Spanish court of King Philip.

***Pope Pius V** addressing **Ambassador Zuniga** (Spanish Ambassador to the Holy See),* "My dear Ambassador - it is with great humility that I receive your acquiescence to join with our besieged Venetian brothers in a League formed to thwart the Turk from continuing their reign of terror and conquest throughout the Mediterranean.

Nonetheless, may I remind the ambassador that he has kept me waiting for many months in his contemplation. Since March 7th, the feast of St. Dominic, to whom Our Lady gave the Rosary, have I waited. At this late date I can only commend the cause into her hands. As such, in addition to requesting that Don Juan assume command of the fleet, my sole request will be that all soldiers and sailors be given a Rosary, and that it be their daily supplication for victory."

Ambassador Zuniga replies, "Your Holiness, it is my sacred honor and duty to convey your wishes to His Sacred Majesty, King Philip; even so, I solemnly assure you that our allegiance is not only with you, but the entire League in this noble and necessary venture. You humble us with your holding of Don Juan in such high esteem."

Pius V acknowledges, "Philip is a loyal and faithful Christian king; he has many concerns in many dominions.

But Don Juan is unburdened by concerns of state; he has demonstrated a fidelity and wisdom beyond his years and the courage and leadership of his royal lineage. Truth be told, it is not hard to believe that Philip might bear a mite of jealousy for a half-brother as highly acclaimed as Don Juan.

Though I have not yet met him personally, I have read the first-hand accounts of Don Juan's devotion and valor in defeating the uprising within Spain.

His personal leadership of men in the rescue of the knights of Malta against a far superior enemy force show not only his personal bravery and devotion but his solicitude for the men under his charge – the mark of one far older and wiser than his years or youthful exuberance might suggest – Yes – he has the right blend of bravery and wisdom –

I believe that his youthful ardor will embolden our side with courage; and with righteous might.

He is the one chosen to end the scourge which for decades has raped, pillaged, terrorized and enslaved the poor people of the Mediterranean. Famagusta was the spark which has lit the fire in the people.

Don Juan is the flame which enkindles the souls of men and inspires them to carry forward the torch to Victory.

**Furthermore, he is a true descendant of the Holy Kinship –
from the lineage of St James. This is a Papal secret to which
you are now entrusted; that the Pope must always know the
true lineage of the Holy Kinship – that is, the line of
descendants from the sisters of Mary Our Blessed Mother. The
children of her sisters, though cousins of our Divine Savior
were often actually referred to as his brothers – including St
James himself!"**

Ambassador Zuniga in full acknowledgement, says, "Your
Holiness, all else pales before the prospect of victory which Don
Juan inspires to his very soul."

Pius V agrees, "d'acquerdo my son"

IV – Mary Queen of Scots

In order to increase the ranks of soldiers and sailors to fight on the side of the Holy League, Don Juan had agreed to be taken to a secret location in Scotland for a clandestine meeting with Mary Queen of Scots. As he arrived, he was struck by the dedication of her royal entourage - it was clear that they would give their lives for her.

Upon seeing Mary, he was also immediately reminded not only of her beauty but of her intelligence and humility.

Mary greeting Don Juan says, "My dear Don Juan I am truly privileged among the female persuasion of Europe to be in the presence of such a chivalrous prince.

Since the unfortunate death of my young husband, King Francis, some have said that ours would be the political marriage of the millennium, but I say to you that I am not even worthy of your attention. Rather your cause matters so much more, well beyond the fate of any individual or their earthly kingdom."

Don Juan, replies, "My Lady, your wisdom belies your age. Please give me your blessing as we go forth – expecting to be greatly outnumbered by the forces of the Grand Turk.

Not only will their forces be far more numerous, but greatly more experienced in navigating the waters and conducting battle at sea."

Mary replies, "My Lord, I will certainly give you my blessing.

Beyond that I will commit the members of my loyal following to your great effort.

Naturally I must dispatch them in total secret; they will come to you and your brother Philip under the guise of an independent force – ostensibly bearing no connection to my person."

Thanking her Don Juan replies, "My dear Queen Mary, I know the danger that follows you every day. Your sacrifice to allow your followers to accompany our cause is the most noble act imaginable. I would be truly honored to have your hand in marriage."

Mary demurs, "My dear Don Juan, you clearly are aware of my precarious position even within my own kingdom. My cousin Elizabeth will not rest until a final solution is contrived, thereby depriving me of my rightful accession to the English throne. Hence, while it is I who would be honored to accept our betrothal, there is only one way for this to come to pass."

Don Juan asks her to make clear, "Please tell me my Lady – how can my dream come true?"

"It may be too much even for you my dear Don – It would be nothing short of the reunification of Christendom. "

Endearing himself to her further – Don Juan prepares to go away sad – but she tenderly encourages him.

"My dear Juanito – we must devote ourselves and all who accompany us – to prayer – indeed our supplications should be directed to Our Lady – Queen of Heaven – she is our true Queen – she will intercede for us before the Throne of God. Think of the miracles that Our Lady has brought about at *Guadalupe in the New World.*

By ourselves, we can accomplish very little; but with heavenly help we can accomplish the unimaginable!

If a great victory can be achieved against the Grand Turk perhaps that could be the catalyst which puts Christendom on the path of reunification. My sincere hope is that it will help my cousin Elizabeth to know that the far greater cause than that of our own affairs of state are those of the Kingdom of God."

In awe of Mary's devotion Don Juan replies, "Mary, you know how unlikely it is that Elizabeth would ever relinquish or share power with you; yet dear Queen, you risk your life for the greater good. I hereby solemnly pledge my life to you. Even if heaven allows a Victory for us against the Grand Turk, if we cannot be together in holy matrimony, I will never take another for my wife."

V – Preparation

At Barcelona – loading the great ships and Galleys of the Spanish fleet, Don Juan is accompanied by Giandrea Doria overseeing the loading of provisions and interviewing soldiers.

Don Juan (looking bright and bold) Addresses Admiral Giandrea, "the beautiful sea beckons us to an historical encounter with destiny – ah – Glory."

Giandrea Doria, looking sad and burdened with the weight of the task ahead, replies "Excellency, I'm told that your chivalrous conduct in personal combat is as unmatched as your passion – but our great force of brave men and powerful ships will seem meager against the grave peril ahead."

Don Juan reassures the Admiral, "we will engage them with a pure heart, determination of spirit and faith in the Holy Mother of our Lord to lead us to victory."

Meanwhile Commanders are interviewing prospective soldiers and sailors where a long line has formed on the dock.

First Soldier, "I have fought in three previous campaigns."

Commander replies, "Any at sea."

Soldier answers, "No sir – but my marksmanship with the arquebus is well-known."

Commander signs in the first soldier and asks, "who's next."

Sailor walks up

Commander interrogates him, "Experience?"

Sailor says, "Yes, my lord."

Commander – "Where?"

Sailor responds, "Venetian Channel."

Commander - looking up warily presses further, "Where specifically?"

Sailor – "Most recently at Famagusta".

Commander (expressing horror) "Famagusta!"

Sailor (with steely eyes staring back at the Commander as the crowd gathers in close to listen) replies, "When our brave Venetian Commander, Bragadino flew the white flag of surrender, only for the hunger of his people suffering at the hands of the siege – He was taken and he was flayed alive – like St. Bartholomew himself – his stuffed skin was hung from Mustaphas's main mast and sailed to sea as his trophy!"

Crowd – horrified – stares back in hushed silence.

Another Commander interviewing.

Commander (incredulously) "You? Senor Cervantes!"

Cervantes replies "Yes, my lord."

Commander (laughing), "You are best left behind to imagine more tales of Don Quixote – the fictional Knight errant."

Cervantes replies, "Sir, my tales are best told when they are only partially imagined…!"

The Commander doubtfully inquires, "For example what real battle have you ever experienced."

"Sir, I recall well the battle of 6 years ago when the last great Grand Turkish armada set their sights on Malta."

Flashback to battle of Malta where Miguel de Cervantes had volunteered his services –

In April 1565 Cervantes is hurriedly helping to prepare the sandbag defenses on Malta and is doing so in conjunction with other soldiers who speak of the terror of the Turkish fleet having sailed into the Mediterranean with Malta as their initial target and to use as a jumping off point for further attacks on Sicily, mainland Italy and even Spain and other European countries.

Cervantes to his cohort Felipe, on Malta, "Once again my friend, Malta must face a mighty Turkish armada sailing straight for Maltese ground zero. Unlike five years ago when panic overcame the island in advance of their arrival and the conquest was an empty victory for them, this time they will find the tip of the spear of our forces awaiting their arrival; I believe that we can hold them off, though it may be a struggle, with a strong reinforcement from the mainland, there is a chance that we can hurl them back from whence they come"

Cervantes' fellow soldier **Felipe** replies, "Well you know that old Vallette as grand master of the knights of St. John is very wise."

Cervantes agrees, "My friend, we will need Vallette's wise guidance for I fear we will not only be outnumbered but despite our holding the high ground at the fortresses of St. Elmo and St. Michael, they will blockade us such that we are starved."

Felipe inquires, "Yes, a siege but why must they concentrate so heavily on Malta."

Cervantes says, "Strategically it is a stepping-stone to greater conquests but symbolically it is a very great prize indeed in that it represents the home of the knights of St John… who are the sworn defenders of the faith"; (*spoken imaginatively with great romantic emphasis*).

Vallette and his entourage now can be seen in the distance riding up to the position near to where Cervantes and his fellow soldiers are preparing the embattlements at the castle of Saint Michael.

Vallette can be seen taking the salute of the officer in command of the preparations.

Vallette's officer in command indicates that he is having the men dig a moat-like trench around the castle that will prevent the enemy from easily accessing the castle.

Vallette approves the technique but also requires that there be a series of embattlements between the moat and the castle itself. He also informs them that the work must be greatly accelerated since the impending approach of the enemy is now just days away. Finally, he gives instructions for an underground approach to the castle so that supplies can be brought despite a siege.

As Vallette rides through the area, great honor and respect is shown to him.

Vallette then gathers his advisors together at his quarters where they are briefed by two spies.

The spies indicate that the Turks will attack in a most unlikely manner from the northwest as well as simultaneously, the southeastern part of the island to take advantage of their naval superiority and storm the island cutting off retreat as well as reinforcement.

Vallette indicates that preparations will proceed accordingly to counter such a strategy.

He then dispatches a courier to coordinate the initial defense of the island against such a strategy with the eventual reinforcement and counterattack.

The eventual reinforcement and counterattack plan was being devised by Philip II and his subordinates, in particular, Don Garcia de Toledo, Don Luis de Requesens, and the Marques of Los Velez as well as the young Don Juan and Admiral Giandrea Doria.

At the brief meeting Philip sees the young Don Juan bound in exuberantly with the report of the spies revealing the plan of attack of the Turks on Malta.

Don Juan exclaims, "My lord we know from whence the Turk will invade Malta."

Philip says to Requesens, "Don Luis – you must be my brother's senior advisor. I pray that, in light of the valuable intelligence we have received today, together you can develop a plan to assemble and lead our forces into action in time to save the great people of the island of Malta from a fate worse than death itself.

Go and keep me informed.

Don Garcia will remain with me while Admiral Doria will be responsible to you both for naval undertakings and Los Velez for the military forces under your command. Be swift, for the valiant Maltese will be dependent upon you for countering the attack and stemming the siege which will threaten to choke off their very existence."

As the flashback to the scene at Malta unfolds the approach of the black ships of the forces of Mustapha Ali Pasha and his second in command Aluch Ali can be seen on the horizon.

Mustapha Ali Pasha had commanded the victorious Turkish legions in Hungary and Aluch Ali was a Christian apostate who had once been a monk in Italy.

As the black ships approach Malta, the sun begins to set and Mustapha signals Aluch Ali to set anchor and come aboard the flagship for a meeting.

Aluch Ali – commanding his slaves;

"Acknowledge the signal of my lord Mustapha. See to it that our anchor is dropped and prepare the rowboat."

Aluch Ali boarding the row-boat commands, "swiftly now, we must not keep his Excellency waiting" as they row.

He orders they be lashed, and the six slave rowers respond by powering the boat through the water to the flagship; but griping amongst themselves.

Aluch Ali announces, "My poor Christian slaves, don't you enjoy your inferiority to those who will soon conquer and rule all of Europe?"

Aluch Ali's assistant says, "Excellency, we will soon have many more such as these slaves. We have only to continue our customary conquests to put their services to good use."

Arriving at Mustapha's vessel they climb aboard and enter Mustapha's cabin to find a dark room but lavish spread; And Mustapha welcoming Aluch Ali and his assistant;

"My good men, please indulge your desires here at our table; let us drink and dine in anticipation of another great victory for our noble Selim."

Aluch Ali replies, "My lord, your plan to attack simultaneously at opposite corners of the island is a brilliant one which will cut off all retreat."

Mustapha Ali Pasha says, "Ah yes, however one small change must I reveal to you this night; my attack in the southeast will take place immediately in the morning while you will sail around the island and attack as soon as you can; probably, with a good wind, in three days you should be able to attack in the northwest cutting off the Maltese retreat."

Aluch Ali answers, "brilliant, clearly we have the advantage of superior strategy, tactics and the element of surprise which will lead us to prevail again."

In the predawn hours of the following morning the Turkish attack is launched on the southeastern section of the island of Malta. The initial assault is incredibly brutal as the Turks are quickly within the outer defenses of the island's fortifications. In the action Cervantes is taken prisoner and thrown in with the other captive Christian galley slaves to man the oars of the great Turkish ships.

Nonetheless, the Turks' initial success is followed by their advance grinding to a halt at the castle of St. Michael where Vallette had the foresight to expand greatly the forward fortifications.

Vallette with his group of subordinates are found discussing the siege by which the Turks have been starving the three holdout castles on the island of Malta.

Vallette announces, "It's been four months since the Turks landed here on the island of Malta. We grow weaker by the day. Our three forts have even been cut off from each other by virtue of their discovery of our underground tunnels."

Captain Girard Bertrand, Vallette's chief of staff, replies, "Your Excellency we have made a noble and steadfast defense of the island; unlike their last incursion when surrender was rapid. Can we not sue for peace? To relieve the suffering starvation of the people."

Vallette in a fatherly way answers, "My dear Bertrand I too have been on the verge of despair at the suffering of our people. Their valiant courage has been the only vestige of strength I have had left to draw upon for sustenance."

Colonel Azarias, commander of the garrison of the castle of St. Michael, responds, saying, "My lords, I have a plan to propose that may serve to facilitate our rescue by the Spanish relief forces under Don Juan."

Vallette replies, "Please share your thoughts with us – esteemed colonel."

Colonel Azarias says, "My plan is a simple one: at each of the castles a small group can be formed to escape through the lines of the Turks.

The groups can rendezvous at a point to regroup and further fine tune the plan – to form scouting parties to reach the rescue forces of Don Juan – in this way the forces of his highness will know where best to counter-attack. Indeed, there should be multiple attacks simultaneously on the Turkish strongholds – they can also indicate which of our outposts are most in need of aid."

Vallette agrees, "it's so simple as to be brilliant! Can the initial communiqué of the plan be conveyed by infiltrating a messenger through the lines or must it be by smoke signal? Yes, perhaps that is the safest method.

But the plan will require great daring."

Captain Bertrand responds, "My lord, as I am a bachelor with no family to fear for my life, may I volunteer to lead the bandoliers."

Vallette reluctantly answers, "My son, you know how much I need and value your services as my assistant - but you are called to a higher purpose – so how could I refuse your gallant offer - the task is yours."

The ensuing smoke signals can be seen being sent and the respective bands of four being formed.

The groups chose a night with no moon for making their escape through the Turkish lines – Captain Bertrand in the lead of the group of four escaping from St. Michael's castle. They rendezvous at a point on the rocky coast with each of the other two groups of four, where there is a boat waiting for them to sail toward the mainland for the meeting with Don Juan.

After almost being discovered by the Turkish sentry they are able to make their successful escape, though one of the twelve falls from the rocky cliffs and is lost.

Upon completing the difficult and arduous sea journey, though greatly exhausted and short of food, they are put on the path to a meeting with Don Juan and his forces by a network of sympathetic townspeople who fear that they will be the next victims of the Turkish route to conquest.

Captain Bertrand – upon his introduction to Don Juan exclaims– "My lord it is my great honor and privilege to meet you…."

Don Juan, cutting him off, "My good Captain – it is indeed we who are given a great gift in receiving you and your group. We know of your sufferings and only wish that we could have hastened our arrival."

Gesturing to his assistants to bring new warm clothes, food and water to Bertrand and his men, Don Juan continues, "And now Captain, while you and your men recoup your strength let us not waste a moment in preparing the rescue of the good people of Malta."

The intelligence developed through the discussion with Captain Bertrand and the various representatives of the respective besieged forts enabled a superior plan to be formulated for the assault on the Turkish forces and the rescue of the valiant Maltese.

Meanwhile Miguel Cervantes suffers to the point of death as a galley slave under the cruel whippings of the Turkish taskmaster – with the drummer pounding out his "battle speed cadence" – to intercept any enemy vessels being sent by Don Juan.

The allied attack proceeds such that Don Juan's ships land a large force on the northeastern section of the island. This was the location least expected by the Turkish forces since the overland route to the besieged Forts in the southwestern part of the island was the longest and most perilous.

Nonetheless, Don Juan's forces were inspired beyond normal human strength to aid their brethren on Malta. Furthermore, they were supplied and outfitted with sufficient supplies and mules to carry them over the difficult terrain. Through their network of spies, the Forts were alerted as to the time of arrival of Don Juan's forces so that any final strength that could be mustered would be summoned for the final expulsion of the Turks from the island of Malta.

The greatly surprised Turkish troops eventually were overwhelmed by Don Juan's stampeding forces: who were greatly aided by the intelligence received on their fortifications and positions from the besieged Maltese' spies. Though the battle was brutal it was much less than would otherwise have been the case without the element of surprise.

Indeed, as the Turkish land forces are being attacked; the Turkish ships are brought in to evacuate their troops to escape annihilation by Don Juan's forces.

In the chaos Cervantes, and other galley slaves manage to escape captivity, and reach the safety of a concealed shoreline location.

Cervantes catching site of Don Juan commanding his forces in battle as they attacked the Turkish position in front of the castle of St. Michael marvels at the grand spectacle of the dashing Don Juan bravely exposing himself to enemy arquebus fire as he leads from the front.

Cervantes remarks, to his captive comrade – "look at the great Commander on the Hill – he has planned a gallant assault with stealth and skill. His men are brave under his leadership and inspiration to relieve our great suffering and restore our dignity. Thank God for his chivalrous saving hand. Someday I will write of their heroism to save us, their brethren. For now, let us rally to assist in our own redemption."

As they break out of their concealed position, they charge forth toward the fort to join in the attack on the Turkish forces.

Afterwards there is a great victory celebration with Don Juan riding in the center to the cheers of the great multitudes; but in his humility he submits to Vallette; placing the sword of the conquered Turk on the table before Vallette.

Don Juan says, "My dear Vallette, you have earned this honor; valiantly leading the people of Malta to withstand the terrible torture of the four-month long siege. May God continue to bless you and the people of Malta."

Vallette replies, "My son, thanks to you and your brave leadership we have lived to give glory to God another day. I am old but from what I have seen, I believe that you are destined to carry on the tradition of the Maltese people; perhaps even to spread the resistance to tyranny and torture throughout the whole Mediterranean and all of Europe. We shall have a great celebration where you will be our guest of honor."

After Mass, giving thanks to God for their survival, a great celebratory feast is held in Don Juan's honor where he is proclaimed an honorary Knight of Malta. Many ladies were smitten by his handsome looks and charming manner.

<u>**VI – Plans for Embarkation**</u>

Arriving to the staging area; King Philip and his cortege joined together with the senior expedition commanders in their final prepatory War Council before embarking of the great fleet. Among the commanders are:

> *Don Juan*
> *Don Luis Requesens*
> *Don Garcia de Toledo*
> *The Marques of Santa Cruz*
> *Admiral Giandrea Doria and*
> *Sebastiano Veniero, a Venetian who was governor of Corfu and Crete.*

Don Juan opens the meeting by addressing the King, "Your Highness, with your blessing we must make haste to link forces with the Venetians before the fall storm season."

Requesens retorts, "With all respect my Lord, it is even more critical to preempt the enemy from gathering further strength. If we embark now, we can accelerate the preparations of the Venetians and perhaps engage the enemy before they can gain the open sea beyond Famagusta."

All are hushed at the mere mention of the place at which one of the great atrocities of all time had recently place.

King Philip replies, "Yes, my noble lords, I do understand and acknowledge your urgency and request for immediacy of action. Yet proper preparation, especially the recruitment process can mean all the difference in such an action in which we are sure to meet a far superior-sized force.

My emissaries even now are sending word throughout Europe, of the impending engagement. All will know and those who can and must fight will not forsake this great chance to defend Honor and righteousness. Even so, we do not seek an angry, disorganized mob bent on vengeance, but a strong cohesive force, composed of individuals who possess the ardent desire for personal and collective victory. Sadly, those who have lost family, friends, children and wives, to the ever-widening advance of the Grand Turk, are the best candidates.

Now, at the end of July, let us target six weeks from today as the date of embarkation."

Sighs of disappointment emanate from all, but most of all from Don Juan.

King Philip says to Don Juan, "My dear brother - your time will come - Let us not fall subject to young impetuousness. Rather avail yourself of the wisdom of those seasoned commanders who now surround you."

The training exercises and preparations went on laboriously during the ensuing weeks.

The men trained in personal combat as well as in group engagement.

<u>*VII – Turkish Court*</u>

*At the Court with the Sultan **Selim, Mustapha Ali Pasha** and **Aluch Ali**, the senior Turkish leaders conduct a Council of their own.*

Selim opens the meeting saying, "My brothers - I have summoned you in such secrecy because I sense the presence of spies who report our anticipated actions to that most inferior King of Spain, Philip the II.

While our forces have known only victory against such inferior foes, we must not allow our enemies to plan so well as to counter the final and inevitable thrust of our conquest as they did so well at Malta.

We must be sure that they remain demoralized and dejected so as to be satisfied in subservience upon our final ultimate victory.

In the aftermath of our victory at Famagusta on Cyprus - they are on the verge of crumbling. We are crushing their will to stem the onslaught through our superior tactics, fearless fighting and tremendous and painful punishment for those unwilling to accede.

One more bold strike and I will rule all the Mediterranean - indeed then the whole world - My question is, what should be the next point of attack - should it be the tall tower of Venice, or Spain or even Rome itself?

Whichever we choose, we must feign the attack in another direction."

Mustapha Ali Pasha adds, "Great one - the stars are aligned in our favor, and we should continue the assault along the lines of the stepping stones - They are expecting that our reach will now engulf Rome - while we can feign such - we should instead wheel our main attack on Venice. When an unsuspecting Venice falls - the three-pronged stool can stand no longer."

Aluch Ali advises, "Great Selim, my wise Ali Pasha gives good counsel - but my men are eager for the prize - until now we have been viewed merely as blood-thirsty pirates. If we can swiftly conquer Rome, no other battles will be necessary; the wealth of Venice and the servitude of Spain will be within our grasp."

Selim replies, "My wise ones - you give good counsel - I will render my decision by secret sealed order to be revealed only after sail has been set."

While preparations are made - the reign of terror must be brought to a crescendo to strike fear in the hearts of all Christendom!"

Ali Pasha exclaims, "Mighty one - I will let you down neither in the matter of the reign of terror nor in the larger objective of complete conquest!"

As Ali Pasha and Aluch Ali take their leave of Selim, Ali Pasha strides past four crucified Christian prisoners on his way to his flagship preparing to set sail out of the Bosphorus with "forty great galleys." All the while, other Christian prisoners can be heard wailing in agony as they are "flayed alive as further sacrifices for victory."

Catarina – a mature, late teenage girl at an orphanage – in the town of Racconigi – with her friends – raggedy and poor in their classroom listen as **Their Teacher, Francesca, instructs her** Girls, "We have a small treat for you. Tomorrow, a great crowd will assemble to see the parade of Don Juan traveling through town on his way to Milan."

Catarina's friend Bernardine Chimes in with great excitement, "I have heard that he is the most handsome and dashing man in all of Europe – not to mention chivalrous and brave…."

Catarina replies, "Certainly his reputation precedes him."

Catarina's friend Isabella dreamily adds, "It takes my breath away."

Catarina replies, "All to what advancement for us? though we are poor – we have not lost our dignity."

Caterina's classmate Marianna says, "What dignity have we ever had – much less you – who came to us so recently since your parents could no longer even provide you a morsel of food to eat."

Catarina, proffering a sad, wry smile says, "It's true we were poor but I'm here not so much from poverty – slowly adding, we were living near Famagusta…" (silence hushes the group) as a flashback to the bloody scene at Famagusta streams into her mind.

Catarina, explaining as flashback occurs to her, "We had a short happy life there – cultivating and raising cattle- we had found a peaceful paradise – they landed on our shore flying the flag with the Crescent Moon; They burned it all – houses – churches; Our people were maimed and slaughtered wantonly with no mercy or quarter – Only those enslaved survived the onslaught – or the very few who escaped…"

Mariana sadly says, "I'm so sorry – we had no idea."

The next morning the parade is held, welcoming Don Juan as he proceeds on his diplomatic mission to Rome.

Don Juan – Handsome and dashing – rides through town with great fanfare – greeting ladies with charm and grace – though with a certain debonair expectation of destiny beyond mere confidence.

Privately Greeting the mayor of Racconigi, Don Juan tells him, "My dear mayor – I must only savor your hospitality for tonight – the mission of diplomacy has taken on a need for extreme expediency – the people were already aware of the atrocities at Famagusta – and now the story of an impending massacre at Corfu has begun to spread among the people – Our people's fear grows while the Turk's confidence for conquest has increased to a near maniacal, superhuman level – Our alliance must rapidly be solidified so that operations can begin to defend the people and eliminate the Turkish threat."

That evening a formal dinner is held in Don Juan's honor and the Mayor's daughter ingratiating herself to Don Juan whispers, "My lord you have truly impressed my wise father with your own level of wisdom and maturity."

Don Juan demurely replies, "Let us not speak of me but let me enjoy your loveliness with a dance – where we can speak more privately."

Meanwhile, Catarina waits on tables with other orphan girls who marvel at the handsome prince.

As the girls swoon over the dashing Don Juan – Catarina sees beyond his appearance and focuses on his sincerity and solemn purpose. ***She dreams of the prospect of stowing away on the voyage; she implores one of Don Juan's Lieutenants….*** "Sir, your mission of diplomacy seems so delicate – how will it ever lead to the defense of our people and lands from the terror that we have experienced?"

Lieutenant Rodrigo replies, "My lady – (speaking to her with great esteem and respect despite her being ostensibly below his station in life), "I know that it can all seem so remote from the very real and serious concerns of those who face or have fallen victim to the Turkish scourge. Nonetheless – for this very reason it is incumbent upon us to form the strongest and most impregnable of Alliances – so that we may never again be terrorized by this menace. We are at the very final moment of securing just such an alliance among the diverse group of proud peoples with disparate interests.

Indeed, the Allies seem to realize that these disparate interests may very well have contributed greatly to the predicament that we face today. I believe that there is a great desire to prevail above these disparities – in such a way as to not have the alliance break down again.

Hence – some would have a certain young man lead the allied forces. However, for agreement on such an appointment a certain young man must be sanctioned by His Holiness – the Pope – but I say too much – Please forget my mere utterances as they are my own personal meanderings and do not necessarily bear any reflection on whatever the reality may or may not be."

Catarina speaking with great admiration, "My lord – you have spoken eloquently – as a true junior statesman – nonetheless, although I take your command to forget your words as a solemn obligation– there are those for whom there are selfish reasons to defeat this scourge…."

Rodrigo responding with the recognition of horror in his voice asks, "Revenge?"

Catarina answers, "Well, surely you must recognize that revenge is an inherent human emotion when there has been such grave injustice… *as at Famagusta.*"

Rodrigo says, "My lady – I don't mean to be callous, but of course you must know that ultimately vengeance belongs to God."

Catarina says sadly, "Yes, my lord – I understand."

Rodrigo replies, "Yet you are moved to deep sadness in your acknowledgement...."

Catarina crying softly; ... "My parents were..."

Rodrigo warmly answers, "Ah, I understand – How cold and insensitive you must think me – only now do I understand why you are at the orphanage...."

The following morning Don Juan and the Mayor are meeting privately as Don Juan's entourage waits to embark for Rome. This would be the final leg of the diplomatic mission to meet the Pope.

Don Juan says, "My lord mayor, you know how important this final leg of my mission is. I go to obtain the blessing of his holiness Pius V, and his agreement to the terms of the Alliance. I am entrusted with a special letter from my brother, his sacred majesty, Philip the II. May I have your blessing for the events which I pray will be set in motion by this momentous meeting."

The Mayor gives Don Juan his blessing saying, "May the Lord lead you to triumph and to safety in your most fateful mission – my son."

Don Juan thankfully replies, "We have been truly humbled by the warm and gracious hospitality you and your people have shown us. I have sensed an undertone of grave concern that your people have for the situation and in turn for our mission. Despair not, there will come a day in the next weeks and months where they may have a chance to join in the mission."

The Mayor somberly says, "Come my son – let us say no more but witness what may unfold...."

The Mayor's daughter scurries in to meet them as they move toward the door of the Mayor's office and pleads, "Don Juan, my lord, how I wish you could stay with us – the people (meaning herself) have been enchanted by your presence – will you not return to visit us again very soon."

Don Juan speaking longingly and warmly replies, "My dear lady, you know that I would surely remain in the embrace of this gentle and kindly place – if only I could. Rest assured that I count it among the most special of places that I have had the very good fortune to visit." (as he kisses her hand warmly).

Don Juan then boldly moves to and through the door to join the others in his "diplomatic" party.

Meanwhile Catarina is in the arms of Rodrigo begging him to stay.

Catarina lovingly begs Rodrigo, "My dear Rodrigo won't you resign your commission and stay here with me?"

But Rodrigo warmly replies to Catarina, "You must not – you of all people know the mission we…."

Catarina endearingly stops him, "…hush, I know…."

Meanwhile secretly she plots to find a chance to stow away as a male servant with them on their mission.

The caravan leaves with Don Juan on his horse, leading the way; he turns to see his Lt. Rodrigo riding rapidly toward him as they link up to lead the caravan on toward Rome.

IX Rome

Don Juan arrives at the Vatican – quietly slipping in just as he and
Lt. Rodrigo had planned, arriving at dawn, leaving their entourage
outside the walls of the city of Rome. As they arrive, they are
greeted by the Swiss guards who escort them through the gates of
the Vatican's walls and into the Pope's chambers.

Pope Pius – warmly greets Don Juan, "My son, I have awaited
your coming with great anticipation and thanks be to God for your
safe arrival," and to Lt. Rodrigo "of course, thanks to you as well
my son for accompanying Don Juan safely on the journey."

Don Juan, kneeling, greets the Pope, "Your holiness, (kissing his
ring and trembling in awe of being in the Pope's presence) – I am
not worthy to be here with you," (remains kneeling at his feet).

Pope Pius, helping Don Juan to his feet, warns him, "My son you
must strengthen yourself against any trepidation or temptation; the
task you face is indeed a monumental one.

Nonetheless, God does not intend for these battles and killings to
continue;

As a true descendant of St James – you are blessed as a member of
the Holy Kinship – therefore it falls upon your shoulders – to
defend Christendom and end this fighting with one last decisive
battle….

At long last, bring us peace – Dona Nobis Pacem – Semper Fidelis (the pope thus granting his blessing to Don Juan to protect Christendom).

On your diplomatic journey you may encounter the brethren of my Swiss guards some of whom I understand may wish to volunteer their services to the cause…."

Franz, the commander of the Swiss guard who has remained in the room, speaks up, "Your holiness, my Lord Don Juan, I believe that it is well known how we Swiss are a peaceful and customarily neutral people – many have construed this neutrality as unwillingness to fight, but when it comes to injustice and tyranny – nothing is further from the truth."

Pointing to a sculpture in the room, Franz adds, "Observe here the sculpture that the Swiss have given as a gift to his holiness upon the establishment of his Swiss guard.

It is the image of the dying lion with a spike through his heart. He is symbolic of our true calling of loyalty and friendship; that is, though the Swiss are neutral; when we fight on your side against tyranny and injustice, we fight to the death!"

Don Juan stares up at the sculpture – moved to tears at the thought of the last measure of devotion to their noble cause which he knows will soon befall many….

Pope Pius says to Don Juan, "My son please carry this letter to your brother – his sacred majesty – Philip – in it I have acknowledged a mea culpa of my own."

Don Juan *inquisitively asks* – "Your Holiness? What can you have done?"

Pius explains, "In the face of such grave forces arrayed against us as the Ottoman Turks - I have made the mistake of choosing the wrong timing to accentuate the differences between our peoples and natural allies."

Don Juan still unclear replies; "Your Holiness; I still don't understand."

Pius further elaborates, "In excommunicating Elizabeth, great turmoil has been exacerbated within Christendom to allow a window for our enemies to take advantage of the disunity that our own internal squabbling has caused.

The English people have always been Catholic, and it has been a sad circumstance that royal pride has denied the people the natural affinity for their true religious heritage. This has been of great concern to Philip and to the Holy See. Indeed, your brother's realms have also experienced much distress due to such and other similar turmoil in the Netherlands and the New World where Elizabeth's minions such as Sir Francis Drake have repeatedly raided the settlements. Only the great fortification at Puerto Rico – Ironically named – El Morro has stopped them from overrunning the entire Caribbean.

These are grave concerns but none so immediate as the Ottoman Turks who even now are on the attack in the Mediterranean and are massing to invade Venice; perhaps even Rome itself."

Don Juan acknowledging the threat replies, "I understand Holy Father."

Pius goes on, "My sons, the Lord will guide you, through the intercession of Our Lady of Victory; only in your steadfast dedication to the ultimate cause of peace will you be victorious. God bless you my sons - dismissing them - Franz will have his men see to your safe return to camp.

Don Juan & Lt. Rodrigo – Kiss the pope's ring and receive his blessing.

They leave with Franz, who gives instructions for linking up with and arranging to have a Swiss legion – join the forces of the alliance.

X – Scots Join the Battle

Back at the Spanish royal Court, Philip is anticipating the return of Don Juan from his diplomatic mission to organize and unite the various parties to the League alliance.

Prior to the return of Don Juan - Philip is expecting the arrival of Sir Thomas Stukeley - the Scottish nobleman surreptitiously sent by Mary Queen of Scots.

Philip – *to Stukeley who arrives clandestinely at the Escorial –* "My dear Senor Stukeley, I understand that your Scottish people long to be free of the yoke of the English - much as the Scots achieved their political freedom - due to the spirited resistance movement led by Sir William Wallace."

Stukeley bowing to the King replies, "My Lord, I am no William Wallace; but for the Scottish people that I represent, I am here to seek your help in allowing us to restore our freedom to practice our Catholic faith that we have cherished for many centuries. As you yourself know my lord, we are among many throughout Britain who long to be free to return to our Catholic faith.

Indeed, the British people embraced you when you were wed to Mary; Henry's true daughter from his marriage to your great Aunt Catherine of Aragon. They embraced you at least partially due to Your Majesty's devout adherence to our true faith."

Philip replies, "My dear sir, you may not fully realize the grave nature of the situation Christendom is facing elsewhere in the world besides the British Isles."

Stukeley challenges the King, saying, "I fear that such impending danger emanating from elsewhere in your dominions may preempt your majesty from sending a force to Britain at this time; however, I have a plan which I have reason to believe can achieve the same result.

My people support the accession of Mary Queen of Scots to her rightful place on the English throne. This will support your majesty's desires and perhaps even bring to fruition the much-rumored and heralded marriage of your illustrious half-brother Don Juan to Mary Queen of Scots – and thus the kingdom can rightfully be restored to its one true heritage."

Philip, deep in thought, ponders his reply before saying, "My son, it is true that Her Majesty Mary Queen of Scots is falsely accused and unjustly detained under house arrest by Elizabeth and her minions like Cecil for fear that the people will acclaim her to her rightful place as true heir to the throne of England as well as Scotland. Nonetheless, I must not be involved in any nefarious plots of intrigue at the English court.

However; should you be able to muster enough of your people to form a considerable contingent for my Mediterranean campaign, I will reward you accordingly in the quest to restore our Catholic faith to the British realm, which the people are clamoring for."

Stukeley inquisitively asks, "How my lord?"

Philip replies, "I will take the armada thus formed for the Mediterranean campaign; including your Scottish contingent and re-form it to sit off the British coast as a warning that the Catholics of Britain must be allowed to practice their faith freely."

Stukeley answers, "Sire – with all due respect – do you contemplate more than just the threat of action?"

Philip sensing Stukeley's dedication assures him, "Indeed – I see that you are devoted to the cause! Let us sincerely hope and pray to Our Lady of Victory that success in the Mediterranean is a harbinger that will catalyze the reunification of Christendom – from the continent to the British Isles and beyond!"

<u>XI Final Assembly Toward Destiny</u>

Finally, on July 20th, 1571 - Don **Juan, having completed his delicate diplomatic mission of unification and fully assembled the Spanish fighting force,** weighed anchor at Barcelona; sailing out into the open Mediterranean in order to join forces with the other ships of the allied league.

The Fleet's first stop on July 26th is Genoa - Where a society celebration ball is held in Don Juan's honor, including many eligible bachelorettes. With his charm and manners - not to mention good looks, fine dancing, gallant and chivalrous attitude - all Genoa admired him as their dashing hero.

Upon leaving Genoa in a parade Don Juan is joined by his friend **Alexander of Parma** and together they set sail for Naples as the next rendezvous point for assembling of the allied force.

On August 2nd in Naples - Don **Juan** is seated on a throne on the steps of the high altar - in steel armor, spangled in gold and his shoulders draped with the decoration of the Golden Fleece – symbol of royal stature – is in full view of a huge congregation gathered for Mass.

After Mass - Cardinal **Granvelle** - viceroy of Naples, presents Don Juan with the commanding Admiral's flag and the giant banner of the Crusade, which has been blessed by the Holy Father. The banner is azure blue and depicts Christ crucified with the coats of arms of the Pope, King Philip, Venice and Don Juan at the feet of Christ.

Sailing further along their route toward destiny on August 23rd - Don **Juan** arrives at Messina on the island of Sicily.

He has sent word ahead that since the final assemblage of the League's fleet was to be completed in Messina with the arrival of the Venetian ships - there would be held a Council of all his senior officers - while the vessels are arriving and assembling.

Meanwhile the Allied fleet continues it's search for the Turkish ships.

Don Juan - (addressing the Council) "My Lords - I extend greetings and good wishes from his Sacred Catholic Majesty - King Philip of Spain.

 I have called us together here today that I may know you and we may all know one another better - since our respective commands must be united as one fighting force if we are to challenge and defeat a superior force such as we face in the coming days and so when our final assembly is completed here at Messina - we shall set sail in the following manner - Admiral Giandrea Doria - will lead our Armada out of port flying green banners - Admiral - your number of vessels will be?"

Doria directing his response to the whole Council, "54 galleys, strong and true My lord."

Don Juan replies, "Thank you, Admiral; a truly formidable force!

The following morning - under blue banners - I will take my force to sea. My flagship shall be the Real; our group will take the center of the battle line - Marcantonio Colonna - shall be on my right, sailing the flagship of the Papal States - and Veniero - of Venice on my left.

Barbarigo, with more Venetian galleys will follow and form up as the Third Squadron - under red banners taking the position on my left flank.

Finally, reinforcing our three frontal attacking groups - will be the Marques of Santa Cruz (Don Alvaro) with his 30 Spanish and Italian galleys. They will fly purple flags – when we engage – they shall function as our reinforcements – plugging any gaps between our lines as necessary.

Overseeing this overall effort and all operations of sail reporting directly to me will be Don Garcia de Toledo - my special operational commander.

Now, as you know, we will be greatly outnumbered in vessels and in men as well as in training and experience. The Turk has been mounting an ever-increasing and menacing force for years. However, our spies have been able to uncover their strategy.

Our plan is to attack and draw them into the fight before they can effectively launch their tactics. In addition, we have in store for them a secret, though admittedly untried but dramatic change in our own tactics. Don Garcia please, will you unveil further details of the battle plan?"

Don Garcia de Toledo elaborates, "The plan is to draw the Turk out into open water. When the battle lines are drawn, we must move quickly to strike. Admiral Andrea Doria has devised a new technique whereby we will discard the large metal espolones from the bows of our ships – this will enable us to place our bow guns lower and hit the Turk's vessels below the water line."

Barbarigo, amid murmuring expresses doubt, "So our 'secret strategy' is merely to discard one of our most powerful weapons? The espolones have always been a critical component of our tactics!"

Doria responds, "I have studied their tactics. The Turk tends to maneuver skillfully in close where the espolones are useless and where their overwhelming manpower will crush us. If, however, we can surprise them by being faster and lighter to deliver devastating initial canon fire, we think we will create an early and unsuspected blow from our guns which will be moved to lower decks to deliver the deadly cannonade. Hence this puts us in position such that their superior seamanship can not only be neutralized but even erased as we can quickly seize the momentum."

Even more than the formation of strategy and tactics for the main battle - the commanders were aware of the need to coalesce their diverse groups into a united fighting force. They realized that this could be accomplished only under and through real combat engagements. They knew that the fighting force needed first to fight together before the main conflict or risk all in their only combined joint effort.

The commanders assembled aboard the flagship Real included:

Don Juan himself
Giandrea Doria
Requesens
Don Alvaro- (Marques of Santa Cruz)
Don Garcia de Toledo
Marco Quirini
Barbarigo and
The old Venetian Veniero

The difficulties of forging such a differentiated group into a united force came clearly into focus as Don Juan struggled against dissension among the disparate groups. For example, Don Juan was enraged at Veniero's execution of disobedient troops, nearly demoting him from command. Requesens had to intervene to calm Don Juan, convincing him that Veniero was far too valuable a commander.

Don Alvaro, acknowledging that the force needed to coalesce, took advantage of the absence of the King for the first time, exhorting the members of the Council:

"My Lords a force such as ours can only succeed when it is forged from a disjointed assembly of diverse groups into a stone-cold unified fighting force."

Requesens agreed, "I have ceaselessly thought of this aspect of our force- and what our **tactics** should be- in order to achieve esprit de corps and yet still obey the king's directives.

Our scouts must be sent out such that we can deceive the enemy into engaging our strength- For example: My men tell me that the pirate Barbarossa has been a renegade from the main Turkish force - yet attempting to establish a stronghold at **Tunis**.

We should sail our main assault force such that Tunis and Barbarossa appear to be able to attack our flank - however this will only be a feint - with our main attack force able to close quickly on Tunis and **crush** these corsairs - all the while protecting against the sudden appearance of the enemy's main battle force."

In order for the ships to close in on Tunis – while still protecting their rear and flanks- they must leave Giandrea Doria guarding the rear of the attacking force out toward the open sea. This would leave Don Juan to lead the attack on Tunis – This he did with all the exuberance of his youthful spirit.

(Now) Captain Rodrigo instructed his men, "When the shore barrage is completed be prepared to disembark our shore attack force into long boats, they will set charges on the hulls of the Turkish galleys just below the water line.

My landing party will draw their defenders from the ships so that the charges can be set unseen – after the rescue of the Christian galley slaves – who will then join forces with our attacking men and overwhelm the enemy shore defenses."

Despite continued internal squabbles, elements of Don Juan's coalition forces fight together at Algiers as well as Tunis and other North African and Turkish outposts; gradually earning mutual respect, establishing Esprit de Corps and coalescing into a fine-tuned fighting force.

XII SEPTEMBER 15th – AT MESSINA

Upon final assembly of the Allied forces, including all the late arriving Venetian vessels; the papal nuncio, Archbishop Odescalchi is sent by Pope Pius bearing a large portion of the True Cross. The archbishop goes to each vessel to give a blessing, including giving each commander a relic of the Holy Wood as well as rosaries for each and everyone in the fleet!

Meanwhile Don Juan is calling out, "Men of the Holy League, it was St Isidore of Sevilla himself who prophesied that a great battle was to be fought at Sea under the command of a young Generalissimo – Victory and an end to Terrorism was St Isidore's ultimate prophesy! We have 3 chaplains aboard the Real, including 2 Jesuits sent by Francis Borgia to hear your confessions and bless you individually as you sail.

For now, please accept by my extension, the solemn blessing of His Holiness Pope Pius V!"

The League ships now begin to sail out into the open sea two-by-two with the Papal Nuncio blessing the ships again as they sail past; with soldiers and sailors kneeling on deck to receive the blessing. Don Juan himself is regaled in Golden Armor, positioned prominently for all to see at the bow of the REAL;

As they sail out into blue water, scouts from the leading elements of the Armada circle back to the flagship in fast frigates and report into Don Juan's cabin.

Several scouts panting and out of breath reporting in, exclaim, "Dear Don Juan, our forward elements have come upon a most dastardly find - The men must witness this first-hand!"

A brigantine scout vessel has sailed through with the news of the fall of Corfu and the horrible atrocities perpetuated by Mustapha Ali Pasha upon the helpless Christians who had already surrendered.

On Corfu - Don Juan's forces find that the Turks had been there and burned houses and churches and killed and mangled the bodies of priests, women and children.

The Scouts further inform Don Juan that the Turkish fleet seems to be withdrawing to the Gulf of LEPANTO. However, according to some captured Algerian Corsair pirates, Aluch Ali, the best of the Turkish navigators, - has returned to Algiers with 73 galleys.

The revelation of the atrocities on Corfu solidifies the unification of the fleet; after some brief infighting among the Spaniards and Venetians - on October 1, 1571 there is a stop at Corfu - where all witness the results of the atrocities for themselves and thus the resolve of the fleet is greatly reinvigorated with righteous anger at the atrocities.

Back under sail, Don Juan's Armada, after gaining the open Mediterranean, is now rowing hard, in the face of the strong wind against them, to intercept the Turks before they can regroup in the bay of Lepanto or return to Constantinople to avoid the fall storm season in the Mediterranean which is about to begin.

Even so, despite the belief that Aluch Ali was not there, Giandrea Doria advises against engagement – as he owns his galleys and does not want to see them lost.

Due to this and the fatigue of the men - Don Juan orders that they put down anchor.

In the midnight hours of October 6th into Sunday the 7th of October – as the men row surreptitiously but mightily toward the last known position of enemy galleys – Captain Rodrigo and Don Juan speak of their first action together – Each had fought hard and now they had become inextricably-linked in the quest to conquer the Turkish terror.

In those minutes - Captain Rodrigo mournfully tells Don Juan of the taking of his wife and daughter by the marauders upon the surrender of Rhodes;

"My dear Don Juan – I have never told you before of my quest – As I was out scouting one section of the defensive perimeter around Rhodes – a group of renegade Turkish marauders surprised our settlement's defenders – overran the village – killing the men and taking all women and children as prisoners – That was three long years ago – Perhaps now you can understand how Catarina has reminded me of her…."

Suddenly, at about 2 in the morning on Sunday the 7th of October, as Don Juan lay awake in the cabin of his flagship the "REAL" - the wind reverses direction and begins to blow from the west, increasing to almost gale force. It blows the cloud cover away to reveal a full moon.

Don Juan, quickly seizing the moment, orders his lookouts high up into the crow's nest.

Climbing up to the highest yard arm on the Real – the sharpest lookout – named Maurice – scans the vast easterly horizon – calling out to Don Juan in a loud cry that he can see the Crescent flag of the Turkish flagship, the Sultana, waving in the stiff breeze.

The Turkish vessels have indeed concealed themselves and are regrouping for battle in the shelter of the Gulf of Lepanto!

Don Juan instinctively knows that this is the moment he has been waiting for.

He sends the order down the entire line of great ships to prepare to move into the designated Battle formation.

The great fleet now spurs to life; the crew jumping to their posts, rowing hard again – and sailing fast toward the Albanian coast.

As Don Juan's forces move aggressively into the open sea, the sense of resolve begins to deepen.

As the sun comes flaming up over the Gulf of Lepanto, Doria's lookout spots what at first appears to be a Turkish squadron returning from a scouting trip.

But the news is much worse!

It's actually Aluch Ali, with his 73 Algerian galleys SAILING BACK fast from ALGIERS and moving Into POSITION TO JOIN THE MAIN TURKISH BATTLE FORCE –

Although this is A HUGE SETBACK, it only serves TO STRENGTHEN DON JUAN'S ALL OR NONE RESOLVE THAT THIS IS THE MOMENT TO BREAK THE TURKISH TERROR ONCE AND FOR ALL!

 A green banner is ordered to be displayed by Don Juan as a signal for all ships to form up in final battle formation.

On the command, multiple banks of oars of the Six great Venetian Galleasses dig deep into the sea, driving the enormous ships of the line to their frontal positions - two by two - each a mile in front of each of the three SEPARATE sections of Don Juan's main line of battle.

Not only have Doria's lookouts noticed Aluch Ali's squadron of corsairs and heavy galleys sailing fast to link up with the main Turkish battle force but an additional smaller reserve force of 20 or 30 Tripoli ships is also moving into position

This is enough to cause Doria to sail back to Don Juan in a fast frigate - protesting giving battle to an enemy with such a large preponderance of heavy ships - but Don Juan overrules Doria, strongly rebuking Doria with the command, "NOW is the time to fight, not to talk."

At this point Doria orders that his secret tactics be put into effect. He orders that the remaining front "espolones", be cut away from the fronts of the galleys, as they would be useless in the close hand-to-hand fighting that would inevitably ensue. This would enable the bow guns on Don Juan's galleys to be placed lower to hit the Turkish ships below the waterline. The order is passed down the line of allied ships and one after another the 14-foot-long spurs at the bow of each ship are dropped into the sea.

Don Juan is now again in his Golden Armor and prepared for battle. On his fast frigate he continues to sail perpendicular to the ships of his advancing fleet, exhorting the men with such encouragement as "Valorous soldiers" - humble the pride and avenge the wickedness of the enemy. It is indeed a cowardly opponent who needlessly slaughters valiant prisoners and enslaves women and children!"

As he says this, he has the men unfurl and raise, the Pope's banner of the Holy League - with the giant image of Christ Crucified, prominent for the whole fleet to see clearly.

As the 20-foot high banner is raised high above the fleet and right next to the Blue image of Our Lady of Guadalupe, an **immense cheer erupts and spreads up and down the line from one ship to the next - left and right like a rebounding echo.**

At a signal from the flagship every vessel in the fleet responds by raising up a Crucifix and moving into position.

Don Juan now kneels on the prow of the Real.

The rest of the fleet follows, all together kneeling in prayer. A great hush falls over the allied Armada.

In contrast, the Turkish side advances forward in the shape of a giant crescent moon, all the while yelling blood-curdling howls, clashing scimitars on shields and blaring horns.

At that moment the wind, which had begun to swirl, now shifts again and begins to speed Don Juan's galleys on to the point of attack.

Don Juan addresses the galley slaves "Men – your freedom now beckons – you are now free to fight – if the Lord grants us victory here today – your freedom shall be yours forevermore. So, rise up and join the battle as we sail into the breach!"

Conversely the galley slaves on the Turkish ships are whipped into action. Nonetheless the Turkish ships have lost their momentum, due to the remarkable change in wind direction. Whereas all on the Christian side noticed how their own sails had been tightened with a seemingly miraculous wind, filling them with a resolve and superhuman feeling of invincibility.

Mustapha Ali Pasha, commanding the Flagship Sultana, directly opposite Don Juan fires the opening canon salvo beginning the battle.

Don Juan responds by ordering that fire be returned.

The six great Venetian galleys commence firing their 264 great guns.

Mustapha Ali Pasha now signals to his ships to execute their battle plan.

His strategy is a relatively simple one. As his forces block the entire entrance to the Gulf of Lepanto the plan is to advance and maneuver to flank Don Juan's forces on both ends of the line; then eventually surround and close ranks for the kill.

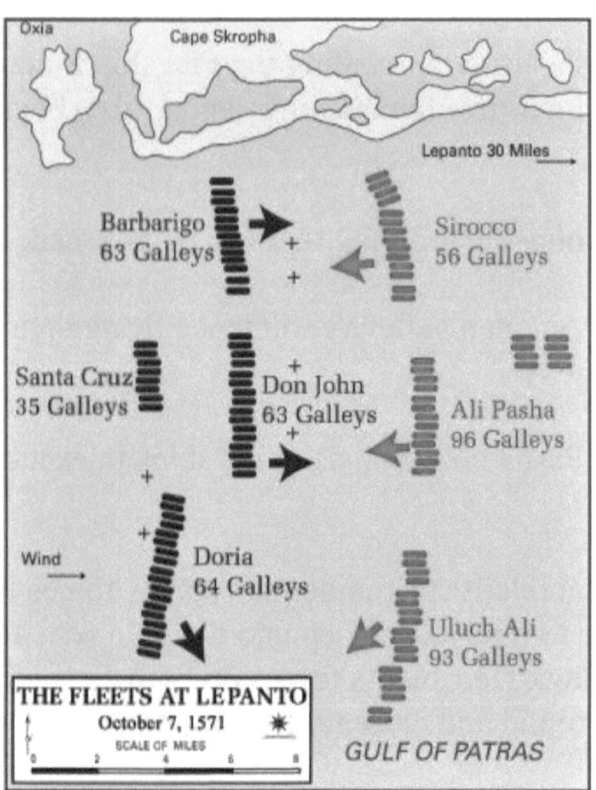

Oxia
Cape Skropha
Lepanto 30 Miles
Barbarigo
63 Galleys
Sirocco
56 Galleys
Santa Cruz
35 Galleys
Don John
63 Galleys
Ali Pasha
96 Galleys
Wind
Doria
64 Galleys
Uluch Ali
93 Galleys
THE FLEETS AT LEPANTO
October 7, 1571
SCALE OF MILES
0   2   4   6   8
GULF OF PATRAS

XIII The Final Battle

Aboard the Sultana, Mustapha **Ali Pasha begins to excoriate his men –**

"Now our moment has come – this battle will the beginning of the end for them – our master Selim has predicted that the Cathedral in Rome will be converted to a mosque and history will mark this battle as the commencement of his prophecy.

Now see to it that our 14,000 Christian slaves row these vessels hard into the breach. If the wind will aid our effort – only a very few of them need be sacrificially slaughtered to serve as examples."

Ali Pasha directly has under his command 96 vessels and is positioned at the center of the Turkish main battle force – exactly opposite Don Juan. Ali Pasha has ordered one of his most capable commanders, Mohammed Scirocco to command the section of the Turkish battle line closest to the northern shore – to Ali Pasha's right as they face Don Juan's forces.

The strategy is to take advantage of Scirocco's ships' shallow draft, get in close to shore where Don Juan's ships, having a deeper draft – cannot sail – thereby enabling a flanking position where the Turkish ships could rout their opponents.

Scirocco's vessels are now racing to gain the flanking position to the north, nearest the shoreline; but Marco Quirini's ships, at the extreme left of Don Juan's battle line takes the Turkish attack head on. Quirini's men fighting fiercely in the breach to defray the Turkish flanking maneuver take on enormous casualties but will not give in. With Quirini urging his men on yelling, "Good men of the Allied force, never give in, keep battling, we must not let Don Juan and the fleet down."

Scirocco's men can't believe the ferocity of the attack on their ships. The experienced soldiers have never seen such resolve in their Christian opponents saying to one another, "What has come over them," as their flanking maneuver fails to overtake Quirini's forces.

Just as Scirocco's men begin to gain a slight advantage in the hand-to-hand fighting, the galley slaves on the Turkish vessels, who had secretly worn away their chains and shackles, at the signal from their leader, break free in unison to pounce on their tormentors. Breaking up the Turkish advantage, the freed galley slaves help to turn the tide. Scirocco himself is killed in the melee. This is the fatal blow. Exhausted and demoralized Scirocco's soldiers can be seen surrendering and begging for mercy.

Meanwhile the massive Venetian Galleasses keep firing relentless broadsides, breaking up the Turkish side's central attacking body.

Don Juan has now moved into a "long boat" for fast maneuverability among his ships. Once again, sailing perpendicular to his battle fleet he exhorts his men; "here is your chance to show your chivalry and to defend the faith…."

As he does so, sailing up and down his advancing battle fleet – enormous shouts of acknowledgment emanate from each vessel as he encourages them onward.

With opposing ships closing in fast upon each other, crack Turkish archers begin launching an onslaught of poison arrows.

Barbarigo, shouting commands to his men, is hit in the eye with one of the arrows and mortally wounded; but as the ships smash and lash together, his men rally in hand-to-hand combat, fighting furiously to fend off the Turks.

Doria, on Don Juan's far right, taking the position to the open sea, is battling the best among the Turkish naval tacticians, the Italian apostate Aluch Ali.

Aluch Ali and Doria have battled before, Ali having won their first engagement decisively. This time Doria's pride is on the line and exhorts his men, "This time right is might and we will prevail."

Aluch Ali is cleverly extending elements of his force far out to Doria's right, in accordance with the overall Turkish flanking plan. This is forcing Doria to string his ships out along the edge of the line, creating a large opening through the ships of the League.

Don Juan, on the Real, observes the precarious position of Doria's ships being strung out far to his right, urgently commands, "Captain Rodrigo, take a long boat, sail over to the Admiral and tell him to close ranks, to prevent Ali from splitting the gap!"

But Doria is not about to obey the order of a junior tactician, he continues to defend against the flanking maneuver, extending his ships further right of Don Juan's battle line to prevent being flanked.

Pouncing on the opening in the line of League vessels, Ali, orders his fastest and best ships to wheel back toward the center of the line. Yelling, he orders, "Whip the galley slaves to Ramming speed."

Crashing through the opening, Ali's ships leave Doria's force isolated at the far right of Don Juan's line.

Heavily outnumbered, by Aluch Ali's remaining ships, Doria's men are being slaughtered, though they are fighting valiantly. Within the first hour, nearly all of Doria's men are killed. The survivors are fighting desperately, valiantly trying to stem the tide but are on the verge of being overwhelmed.

Meanwhile, Don Juan is back at his command post on the deck of the Real. Seeing the carnage of Doria's force, he quickly orders Captain Rodrigo's men, "Devout sailors, you must sail urgently to aid Admiral Doria's group." Once again, Rodrigo's rowers dig their long boat ores deep into the sea, propelling their ships to Doria's aid.

Arriving to the scene, Captain Rodrigo orders his men, "Over the side, join forces with Doria's men."

With the arrival of Rodrigo's reinforcements, Doria's men regain their initiative. Doria can be seen coordinating the combined fighting force. "Together, men counterattack and together and we shall overcome."

Meanwhile, Santa Cruz, commanding the rear reserve, seeing the impending disaster of Aluch Ali's fast ships sailing rapidly through the gap to encircle Don Juan's central force, quickly orders his remaining vessels to cut them off.

Aluch Ali, race to take advantage of his tactics, as his ships get through the opening. His ships brutally attack the lead elements of Santa Cruz' reserves. They are the ships of the famed Knights of Malta who re well-known for their "fight to the death" ethos.

The lead galley of the Knights is the CAPITANA, which directly takes on Aluch Ali.

Aluch Ali commands the men on his seven fast attack vessels, "Now is our chance men, move in for the kill, seize this symbolic Knight of Malta vessel!"

Aluch Ali's men proceed to board, overwhelming the Capitana, killing her entire complement of Knights and their contingent of soldiers.

Aluch Ali commands his men, "Harness the Capitana", let us keep it as another symbol of our conquest."

But Santa Cruz, observing all as he sailed his remaining vessels back to engage Aluch Ali, gave the order, "Engage them, they must not be allowed to sail away with the great ship Capitana, symbolic of the entire order of the proud Knights of Malta."

With Santa Cruz in hot pursuit, Aluch Ali orders his vessels to retreat, abandoning the Capitana.

This was the genius of keeping Santa Cruz' forces with their speedy sailing capability, in the rear as a reserve to plug gaps in the line. This tactic saves the day more than once as Santa Cruz' ships had already fended off Scirocco's fierce encircling attempt at the far left of Don Juan's line.

XIV Aboard the Real

Although the custom of battling fleets at the time was for flagships not to engage directly, tradition was not to be upheld on this day.

Reboarding his flag ship for the imminent moment, Don Juan orders his Maltese Knight sailing master to sail straight for Mustapha Ali Pasha's flag ship, the Sultana, which also is sailing straight for the Real.

Don Juan commands Rodrigo, "Now give the order to those manning the frontal canons on the galleys to hold their fire until they can see the faces of their Turkish counterparts; be sure that they remember their practice drills and aim low; timing their shots to hit as the enemy vessels rise up in the water so as to hit below the water line."

Up and down the line the order is given to remember their practice drills in this regard. He also gives the order to standby to drop away any remaining espolones.

In order to maintain some element of surprise, Don Juan had delayed giving the order to cut away the remaining espolones. Now they are dropped into the sea, further enhancing the speed and firing effectiveness of his great galleys.

As this ensues, **Don Juan exclaims to his staff**, "look how our canons are ripping gaping holes at the waterline. Now my men that we are in range let them have a volley of arrows."

As the men form up to commence firing their arrows, Don Juan notices a strange and small looking person who has joined the barrage.

Don Juan asks Rodrigo, "how can such a small man be powerful enough to fire such a heavy weapon?"

Rodrigo reluctantly replies, "My Lord - I learned only this morning that we had a stowaway – I fear that you will not believe me when you too learn… It is Catarina – and you know what happened to her family – she has been practicing her marksmanship to the point where she is among the best archers."

Don Juan is Incredulous to hear this, replies "Should she not be sent below decks…."

Rodrigo tells Don Juan, "She would rather die than miss this chance to vent her righteous anger…."

Don Juan says, "Nor will I be the one to deny her the chance…We must not lose the initiative."

As the Real and the Sultana come crashing together, the damage to Don Juan's flagship is heavy, with the front of the Sultana crashing all the way through to the 4th line of rowers.

As the emboldened Turks are massing to board the Real, they are impeded by yet another new innovation; a concept introduced by Giandrea Doria for close-quarter combat – boarding nets, which prevent the Turks from boarding the Real in the position where they are prepared to do so.

Instead Don Juan's men (and woman), are assembling behind the foredeck – (where they cannot be observed) – thus they are able to quickly find the most vulnerable point on the Sultana before boarding.

This further takes the Turks by surprise with heavy casualties to the Turkish forces inflicted. This tactic is followed all up and down the clashing lines of opposing vessels. Cervantes himself arises from his feverish, wounded condition to rejoin the brutal fighting.

Mustapha Ali Pasha himself is fighting furiously and valiantly as his flagship is attacked. He can be heard imploring his men to adapt to the change in tactics and move quickly to defend their vessels from the stampeding onrush of Don Juan's forces.

Two times, Ali Pasha's screaming soldiers come charging onto the Real, penetrating all the way to the main mast and wounding Don Juan severely in the foot. Horrific and brutal combat continues with the decks of the Real and the Sultana as well as all ships awash in a bloody, sticky mess.

Attacking repeatedly, Don Juan's men are repulsed two times from the main mast of the Sultana, each time steadily eroding Ali's flagship's defenses.

By this time, the troops of the Real are nearly in a state of frenzy as they sense that victory is within their grasp.

In conjunction with the reinforcements brought up by Santa Cruz, Don Juan's men storm the Sultana, freeing the Christian galley slaves in the process.

At the climactic moment, a bullet from one of the Spaniard's weapons, wounds Ali himself, who falls to the deck, leaving him in perfect position for a freed galley slave to hack off his head; lifting the head up on a spear for all to see. This was the demoralizing moment for the entire Turkish fleet, to the point of despair of defeat.

Don Juan, struggling to walk, announces to his men to retrieve the banner of Christ Crucified from the Real and raise it up the flagpole of the enemy masthead! It was undefiled! A great reverberating Victory cheer resounds up and down the Christian fleet as the banner is raised up the flagpole of the Sultana!

Pope Pius, at the Vatican, is convening a group of cardinals. He suddenly, excuses himself from the table and going to the window, has a premonition of victory, telling all that "our Fleet has just won a Miraculous Victory; let us go and pray in Thanksgiving that this be the end of the torment and beginning of a lasting Peace!"